LIFFEY SWIM

First published in 2014 by
The Dedalus Press
13 Moyclare Road
Baldoyle
Dublin 13
Ireland

www.**dedaluspress**.com

ISBN 978 1 906614 97 3

Dedalus Press titles are represented in the UK by
Central Books, 99 Wallis Road, London E9 5LN
and in North America by Syracuse University Press, Inc.,
621 Skytop Road, Suite 110, Syracuse, New York 13244.

Cover image by Stephen Ledwidge, with thanks.

The Dedalus Press receives financial assistance from
The Arts Council / An Chomhairle Ealaíon.

LIFFEY SWIM

Jessica Traynor

DEDALUS PRESS
DUBLIN, IRELAND

ACKNOWLEDGEMENTS

Poems from this collection have appeared or are forthcoming in *A Modest Review, And Other Poems, Burning Bush II, If Ever You Go* (Dedalus Press), *Listowel Writer's Week Winners Anthology 2011, New Planet Cabaret* (New Island), *Peloton* (Templar), *The Irish Times, The Weary Blues, The Raving Beauties Anthology* (Bloodaxe), *Southword* and *Wordlegs.*

'The Dead' won the Listowel Writers' Week Single Poem Award in 2011.

'Sin-Eater' was shortlisted for the Strokestown International Poetry Prize in 2012.

'eBay Auction' won the Hennessy New Writer of the Year Award in 2013.

A version of this collection was highly commended at the 2013 Patrick Kavanagh Award.

A Dublin City Council Literature Bursary in 2010 and the Ireland Chair of Poetry Bursary in 2014 allowed me valuable time to work on this collection.

Thanks are due to the following people, whose friendship, encouragement and support have made this book possible: Pat Boran, Jane Clarke, Harry Clifton, Richard Cox, Eithne Hand, Dave Lordan, Tom Mac Intyre, Shirley McClure, Éilís Ní Dhuibhne, Helena Nolan, James Ryan and Liam Thompson.

Contents

ﷻ

I. DODDER

eBay Auction / 11
My Aunt Reads the Tarot / 12
Treasure / 13
Clair de Lune / 14
Arachne / 15
Persephone Alone / 16
The Disappearing Garden / 17
Dodder Blackbird / 18
Nineteen-Fourteen House / 19
The Dead / 20
Letters from Mount Fuji / 21
Sin-Eater / 22
Didja / 23
I Unstitch the Sampler / 27

II. LIFFEY

Liffey Swim / 31
Seahenge / 32
Borderlands / 33
Purgatory / 35
Hamelin / 36
Elizabeth and the Globe / 38
Pearls at Blackfriars / 40
From the Diary of Doctor Jekyll / 41
Human Character / 43

Mitochondrial / 44

Larkin's Beard / 48

The Woman Who Woke into History / 50

Dragon Chasing Pearl / 52

Pearl / 53

Love / 54

Ghost / 55

The Water-Table / 56

III. TOLKA

Scenes from a Poor Town / 59

IKEA Sleep / 60

Fire God / 61

An Education in Silence / 62

Crosses on the Road to Sligo / 63

The New Reality / 64

Synaesthesia / 65

Inner Space / 66

Settlement / 67

Lines on Your Thirtieth Birthday / 68

Summerhill Moon / 69

Leaving My Hands Behind / 70

The Lyrebird / 71

Headline / 72

Egrets in the Tolka / 73

Sackville Place / 74

Blackbird in Ballybough / 75

❧

NOTES / 76

To Billie, Anthony and Declan

I. DODDER

eBay Auction

I sift through treasures of the dead
on brightly-lit pages,
row upon row the items I seek:

pendants with coiled, imprisoned hair,
fading like a doll's to a revenant colour;
grey, with kernel of brown or blonde,

Whitby jet brooches shaped like hands,
pointing the way to death
(whichever way you choose),

and lockets that still hold old photos —
these personal mementoes cost the most.
One discloses a man and a woman,

laughing faces animated through
a sepia fog, in front of a dancing privet.
I hope I might someday be preserved like this,

young beneath the photo's cracked veneer;
inexplicably laughing, free of context,
purely myself, whoever that may be.

My Aunt Reads the Tarot

She frowns at my mother,
fans the cards across our vinyl table cloth.
They make a sound like sighing,
as if they have secrets
too terrible to disclose.

My aunt's face pauses
in its reel of expressions
and we know her son
is off his meds again,
looking for gear in old haunts.

In our steamed-up kitchen,
my cards are always
weeping women, snowbound churches,
meetings on dark evenings
with whispered messages.

One birthday she gives me the cards
wrapped in black silk
torn from a blouse
and they fall behind my bed
among CDs, unread books.

Years pass and they vanish —
our futures stay wrapped in silk.
But the Fool still stands on my dresser;
a young man waltzing
towards a cliff-edge.

Treasure

When I was small I knew
that grown-ups hide their treasure
and so I'd search the corners
of our overgrown garden,
pick through brambles in the back lane,
push my fingers into crannies in the granite walls.

Things I found but have since lost:
a rusted lump of cast iron wreathed in flowers,
a glass bottle-stopper worn smooth
as if by water. A robin's nest, abandoned,
a knot-hole groove in the bannister
the perfect fit for my thumb.

Somewhere, there is a map
of the place these things are hidden.
It may be buried in this flowerbed
among a thousand smashed tea-cups
or folded in this book like a bus ticket
that, when it falls, whispers *keep looking*.

Clair de Lune

I see the moon
and the moon sees me —
my mother's face
over mine,
some long-forgotten evening.

But what has been lost
in the space of those years?

That cool, uncluttered moonlight,
the syllables of song
that settled on us both;
and the clarity of seeing,
being seen.

Arachne

You fly from me in droves,
your bodies transparent —

only I feel our invisible string
grow taught, snap.

Now I see you as shadows under
deep water, making signs,

breathing another element
while I work my weaving-frame

stitching shared memories
into the narrative of our being —

trying to know you as your mother,
knowing I never can.

Persephone Alone

Persephone chose the underworld,
but can't remember why;

it seems this must be so:
the chill air, the ubiquitous damp.

She can't tell you why the sun is gone,
only knows that something in summer —

the grease of sex in the air —
made her disappear into this hollow,

a place to count each breath
and winnow the noise of industry.

There is no god here — it's not like the stories —
no fiery centre where two souls spark,

only a twin who sits with her
on frigid evenings, cold as a mirror,

pale as mercury mistings,
faithful only in his silent pairing

as her breath
maps endless winter on the air.

The Disappearing Garden

Now, we are eucalyptus-shaded,
foxglove-dappled, living half in
and half out of the light,

but when you close your eyes
the garden is no longer there;
attempts to summon it

bring only memories
of churned earth, of a past
when it was unimaginable

and so, opening your eyes
is something like loss in reverse;
the same subtle but bone-shaking shock,
the moment when everything appears.

Dodder Blackbird

The time has come to change our parameters;
this, you say, is the real challenge of loss.

Through your words I hear the blackbird's song
across the valley and wonder what he knows.

Behind that coloratura there is speech, certainly,
some old wisdom told and retold to listeners

among the branches, in nettle-clogged ditches,
in the river beneath the rocks —

and suddenly it doesn't matter that words are lost;
within its imagined corners, the world has broken into song.

Nineteen-Fourteen House

There are aches in these walls;
that much I can feel —
one hundred years of slump and settlement,

the glass in the sashes
casts bleary glances on the garden,
washing the lawn in river-water glamour.

After your first turn —
loping across O'Connell Street —
you came back here

to learn again the grammar of home:
the worn oak of the fireplace,
cast-iron tea-warmers in the grate,

trip hazards: a stair shallower
than the rest, a loose tile,
a visual language disintegrating

and the rooms in your mind,
full since the house was built, emptying —
with no one to fill them again.

The Dead

When we went to her the dead were in the house,
clamouring for space in the cramped kitchen,
poring over her mismatched crockery,
arranged not largest to smallest
but according to some apocryphal code.

They were inspecting the sell-by dates
in the pantry and 'ooh-ing' at her tumble dryer
when I came in. I gave them short shrift —
my sisters pretended not to see them
while I struggled past to put on the tea.

Hours later they were still downstairs,
too rude to visit the bedroom and make conversation.
Instead they rifled the photo album and rattled
the silverware, clattering a polka with her spoons
on the French-polished dining room table.

I didn't want to leave her with them,
so I stayed and they promised to behave —
though they were already into the whiskey.
In the small hours she called for them
and, when her life escaped her,

it shook out its legs like a newborn foal
and found itself part of the herd.
Although she had not welcomed them,
she was happy to partake of the comfort
the dead can bring the dying.

Letters from Mount Fuji

From the top of Mount Fujiyama I send you letters,
written on square pages, then folded

in as many different patterns as a snowflake.
I drop them onto thin air; watch them fall into the world.

Open one. In it is a picture from your childhood.
Look at it: it melts in your hand

like the question I ask you, caught on a breeze,
and your answer, taken by the river to the sea.

Even through this constant, year-devouring snow,
I will always send you letters.

Sin-Eater

He blows on his hands to warm them;
it looks like some ritual, some totem.

Between us, nothing but certainty —
the death-sound in the old woman's throat —

and uncertainty — the priest's whereabouts.
Our whispers summon only a flutter in her eyelids.

Someone mentioned the man down the road
who lives alone, who gives some kind of absolution,

so here we find ourselves with this stout man
in a muddied fleece, who breathes on his hands

and places them on the woman's shoulders.
Tears come first, spilling from her eyes;

those milky shallows that have mirrored us all evening
clear for a moment as he bows his face to hers.

He doesn't look at her tears, allows her gaze to travel
to the ceiling above her bed. Only we invade her privacy.

He says nothing. Not one prayer or word of comfort.
We give him a fifty, and wonder.

Some begin to mutter; one man asks what he did.
He tells us that at that late stage she had no voice left,

so he took her sins upon himself,
allowing her to pity him for all he carried.

Didja

I. Game

We have this game —
except it's not a game
because you find it so annoying —

where I say to you
'didja *ever* think?'
about each crossroad

we've met in our past:
that first night in the pub,
when after years

of pretending to ignore you
I mistook your proffered hand
for something more

(and you didn't mind)
and that night in Sligo
where you asked me to

and *yes I said yes*,
and carried the secret,
an invisible band

tracing its scar on my finger
for not-quite-nine months —
that alchemy of absence

become presence over time;
a process that suggests
its own reversal.

II. *Risk*

All games involve chance;
this imagined
forward mapping

can't unmake mistakes
or darn holes in history —
this I learned

when I uncovered
the photo of my dad
in thigh-high snow,

Tallaght, 1980,
wrapped in 'that
bloody astrakhan',

his new paymaster suit
half obscured by Afghan wool,
up to his knees in snow,

its tint and texture
long forgotten now —
and I wondered:

did he dream of a path
from that place to this
where that snow would dim

not only from his memory,
but from perception itself;
where the years could steal it,

leave him alone
in some gloomy room
with us calling in from the blizzard?

III. Evidence

My grandfather was caught
on the hop by death.
In those shrinking days,

decisions became simple —
a toss-up between
a right-or-wrong choice

or an obstinate wish.
And so he asks one daughter
to take from his belongings

certain papers
which she burns for him
without question.

Does she pause to consider
that in those pages
lives a shadow genealogy?

She doesn't.
The stubborn daughter,
she stands by the hearth

while flames blacken the rules
of his most secret of games
in a ritual of enforced forgetting.

I Unstitch the Sampler

There is a future I have already made
and I am stealing it, fibre by fibre,
from myself.

I take the memories apart, stitch by stitch
and knot by knot,
until the sampler frays

and I can no longer see babies,
bottles, soothers, coffee cups stuck
among the weave.

They all fall down; rubber ducks,
wedding rings, cat collars,
spider-plants,

in a pile of faded silk, and I'm alone,
with a thread in my hand —
no notion where it ends.

II. LIFFEY

Liffey Swim

In the dream, the Blessington Street Basin
fills with the Liffey's stout-bottle waters,
but still the swimmers come, in droves,
on the stray sovereign of an Irish summer's day.

The river courses towards the quays,
turning concrete roadways to canal banks
that shrug their shoulders into dark water;
a man rises, seal-like in his caul of silt, to wave.

At the sluice gate, where the river bends
out of sight between toppling buildings,
a black dog jumps, again and again, into water.

And there, at the edge of vision, my parents,
ready to join the swimmers,
gesture their cheerful farewells.

Seahenge

Pass the tideline, dig the sand
until you find the upturned root-bole,
petrified limbs knotted
like memory's tangled threads —

feel the punch in the notion
that in a time long past, men planted oak trees
crown-down in the surf
to share their leaf-light with those who live below;

release your heart-strung gasp
at the roots of that dark world
emerging from the sea
to drink from living skies.

Borderlands

The stone was nothing to look at;
two foot of limestone jutting from the turf,
but legend said diviners tempered hazel rods
by walking anti-clockwise round it.

When the dig began, the soil disgorged
nineteenth-century pennies,
a miraculous medal, a broken pot —
small loot for a small people.

On the third day, a carving was found.
One man touched it, came away with a gash,
though the stone was worn smooth
by our squalls that ride in from the sea,

and not long before one
fractured his arm driving a pick.
The mood turned, the drizzle began,
but still they hefted earth and gravel

into tarns to puzzle men in ages to come.
The stone grew: green deepening
to charcoal black, as if burnt;
with marks on its sides like rows of teeth.

The mishaps continued.
A farmer lost six lambs to crows,
and a boy, just five, was hit by a car,
but they dug deeper and deeper,

hollowed a passage through the drumlin
in search of the stone's root. On the fifth day
they found an opening in the pillar,
pushed a yard stick in to gauge the depth —

stale air flowed out, a sound like a sigh.
Too late they saw the broken support beam —
a man was crushed, as the walls of the pit
folded over him like a blanket.

But one who survived, the man
with the scar that grinned on his finger,
said they'd found a window,
and, through it, faces like their own.

When they left, there was no more trouble.
The women in our border town
uncovered their mirrors, no longer afraid
of what they might see.

Purgatory

There are no holdings in this stricken country,
only forests that stake eternity's claim,
the trees policing sunlight
through knitted fingers and knotted fists.

When our workmen reach the holy lake
the Abbey lies in ruins —
any poor souls that live here
have found their own road to hell.

With the piling of stone
upon stone, I wish for home;
for the wicker fence, the rooting pig,
the stink of wood-smoke and industry,

but King Henry requires a wall
to separate Heaven from Hell;
a gateway to straddle the banks of time,
to call its bland expanse to account.

I know no matter how sturdy this wall
Purgatory will pour forth,
crashing through the forests
towards the fat rose in its clearing,

changing and ever the same
like the thousand rhythms of rain
that beat out in this terrible place
the semblance of time.

Hamelin

He arrived with the rats,
looked no one in the eye,
just played a wheezing song
on that pipe of his. I didn't like it,
but I was itching from the fleas
that infested our beds
and wasn't easy in myself.

I'd heard the tune before
and called it bad luck
but no one would listen,
so I closed my eyes
and ignored the whisper
that touched its lips to my ear.

⸨

The silence now is worse —
it seems as though our wish
to rid ourselves of pests
has made us cursed;
God has taken all
imperfect things from us,
even those we loved.

When he left I watched a cat
toy with a last rat
and lame its back legs.
I wondered if perhaps
God was watching her
and wished he could speak to her
of the pain of vermin.

Elizabeth and the Globe

It is presented to her as a gift
among so many gifts —

a great plaster orb,
a macrocosmic vision

of the pearls that stipple
her own lace halo.

Its skin has been scarred,
tattooed with a thousand lines

like those that map the faces
of the Indians who crawl

Virginia's own earth
a thousand miles away,

those that demarcate a route
or snare tiny princes

in a tightening patchwork,
a maze of shrunken leagues.

And looking at the globe,
its bright jewel diminished

in her cabinet of curiosities
she feels, not for the first time,

dismay at its meanness,
at the emptiness of this egg,

skin teeming with life
its innards can but echo.

Pearls at Blackfriars

For his Winter's Tale,
Master Shakespeare calls
for a covered stage
with the scent of candle-grease
and orange-peel heavy on the air.

There must be torches
to give movement to shadows
and life to the statue;
and for Hermione's face —
tincture of pearl, crushed.

With this bowl of dust
we'll lacquer her age,
encase her in memory
so only a movement of the mind
might release her,

might absolve
her husband's transgression,
as the jealous moon
flings her light
against Blackfriars slates.

From the Diary of Doctor Jekyll

JEKYLL AND THE WOMAN

She welcomes my Mr Hyde –
almost coaxes him over the threshold,
though he needs no bidding.

At first he is flummoxed by her stance –
willow-thin, yielding, and her movement
as she makes to stroke his matted head.

Her eyes shine like winter sunlight
through the withy-wands of her hair
and my monster slavers and is still.

Some infernal heat
forges a pathway between them.
I open my mouth in time to disappear.

JEKYLL AND THE CHILD

Any act of creation is surely a miracle,
the endurance of the human spirit,
the splitting of the seed, the grafted root.

But in the eyes that peer from the nursery doorway
there is spite, brute intelligence —
the stolen toy, the tantrum, the dirty face.

I excuse myself, wander to the garden
to watch the swallows skim the grass;
their blind flight finding its fill without malice.

JEKYLL'S CREATION MYTH

Somewhere in darkness is a dream of water;
from it crawls the lizard that coughs up the sun.

The sun gives the gift of leaves,
exhaled from the light and breathing it in turn.

The lizard eats the leaves, and grows green,
and from the leaf-shade comes man, the world's pet,

but inside him live many worlds and many mirrors
distorting him so that his smile becomes a grimace

because even in the waking world
the darkness is dreaming still.

Human Character

'On or about December 1910, human character changed.'
— Virginia Woolf

Perhaps there was snow falling *on all the living and the dead,*
but you would not approve of that.
More likely London wrapped itself in a moving cloak of rain,
omnibuses swayed like elephants,
glamorous in bounced-back light.

But what changed for you that morning?
Did you wake again as a man or a woman
or find a way to channel all you saw
into those hard black symbols,
those stones that lined your pockets?

Whether you overlooked a city
shrugging sleepily from fog,
or the country's levelling mists,
you must have seen some subtle change;
the glint of water, an inescapable river.

Mitochondrial

I. ESJA'S SAGA

The first settler men were Norse,
the women, Irish —

a pale-haired man tells us
of Irish Esja's saga,

points at her home across the bay
among the wet-footed mountains.

I look for her face through the drift
of passing aeons,

but she vanishes from sight
like a seal in green water.

The man speaks of Thingvellir:
thing meaning *place of law* —

like the old *Thing Mote*
on maps of Dublin,

how it's shared linguistic foot
makes a time-bridge,

a causeway long buried
but lit for a second

by the shared DNA
of a thousand dead Esjas;

Yggdrasil flaring
in crepuscular light.

II. The Viking Wife

In school books the Viking Wife
was always thick-plaited —

apple cheeks blushed red
in her sea-shell face.

She offered a plate of bread,
her homely skill the obverse

of the rape, the slaughter,
all bloodiness exported

to the shores of neighbouring lands
where the surf foamed pink.

But Iceland tells a different story;
dull-haired Celtic wives,

noses running with cold,
faces like slapped arses,

bawling with rage
at their dead Irish men

as they were dragged
to this wind-whipped rock.

Now when I recall the books
the ice-floes clear

and Esja stares from the pages
a thin-faced girl,

her cola bottle full of beer,
hair scrawled back in a ponytail,

her Norseman dead.
The scrapings of this rock *hers,*

the birch scrub behind her
on fire in the night.

III. HALLGRÍMSKIRKJA

The Icelandic elders
built their church

from the body of a whale
thrown from the bay

by God's thunder.
From the green depths

she brought icebergs
and plankton tattoos

to mark her basalt walls
with sacred text.

From her bones
they built the organ,

to sigh its krill-song
to her sisters in the bay.

From her skin
they wove carpets,

so fine and sea-blue
that when the sun shines

an ocean moves
among those who pray,

on their feet,
to the god of sailors

stranded, now,
on a melting inland sea.

From her oil they made
seven lamps that will burn

until the end of days
when the chosen will file

between her ribs,
into her belly

and be carried back
to the glacier's heart

to swim, as the last ice melts,
uncharted depths.

Larkin's Beard

When the time came to stitch
the tapestry commemorating
1913 and its Lock Out,
controversy broke out
over Larkin's beard.

You see, it was a fake —
worn to disguise him
as he addressed the crowds
from the window
of the Imperial Hotel

and when the DMP men came
to take him away,
in the famous photo there's
the beard, sat on his face,
shrouding that big mouth.

But when Bobby Ballagh's
sketches arrive
for us to work up —
Larkin is beardless.
Our sewing circle sits —

stares from photo to sketch,
from long-jawed Larkin
to the bearded gent
of historical fact.
We decide to sew on the beard.

Each strand is stretched
taut through the cloth,
fingers are pricked,
hardened, tendons pulled,
but it is *truth* we're sewing —

we follow the weave
of history, bond over
our small rebellion
as we contour the moustache,
gradate our silks from black to grey.

When the woman
from the committee comes
and sees the beard
she is horrified
by its hirsute challenge

to the narrative
we have been told to represent,
and we all get a lecture
on artistic licence
before the beard is unpicked.

The Woman Who Woke into History

It was an ordinary morning in 1940
when she was struck
by the two thousand years

between the Neolithic road
and the Bronze Age tombs,
smacked by millenia of Christianity —

before which no one
worried if their God
was Catholic or Protestant.

The weight
of these shifting definitions
ploughed her into the ground,

between post-holes and hearth-stones,
where for a moment she saw
the thin line of it all,

glinting in the barrow
like a whisper of sunlight
on the shortest day

and she was awake,
in the midden-rich dark,
until the rampant squaddies

in training for the churning
of blood and bone and sand
rolled their tanks over her,

right through the pathways
of her new archaeology
and she forgot it all again.

Dragon Chasing Pearl

How must it have been that day —
you cutting ribbons from the sky

to weave through clouds —
seeing her below, pearl, or *cleanness*,

the inverse of your starbursts,
your firework displays?

Many have been lost in her surface,
gently eschewing, as it does,

all stain, any reflection but one bent
into the curve of her understanding.

Now wound around her,
I know you by your absence;

a whiting or darkening of light,
that pulsar rhythm.

Pearl

Now we no longer have the pearl,
it becomes difficult to invoke
as anything more than smooth white sphere.

But it couldn't be just that, could it,
this thing we held together and cherished
as if something beautiful and new

might crack through its skin and smile at us,
congratulating our small act of creation?
No, it must have had something swimming

in it, deep below its surface,
sliding through its powdery depths,
something that knew us.

Otherwise, what was the pearl
and why did we hold it so carefully
like a flour baby or a cossetted egg

used to prepare a boy and a girl
for all the future and history
a touch can spark?

Love

Of all the letters
in the word 'love',
only one is fit for a gift;
not 'l' the divider,
'e', the maze, or 'v',
the two-fingered goodbye.

I make for you an O,
the vulnerable O
of lips that enfold
the welcoming spaces
at the centre
of sharp-angled words.

My gift for today,
this O: the iris
of the word I offer
opening silently
to look at you.

Ghost

I decided we should spend the day together
and so you stalked me through clothes-rack forests;
a silent hunter.

When we emerged into the evening for drinks,
you began to speak; a tumble of words
fell from the hard line of your mouth,

unfrozen now, unfixed, and every word we'd never said
hit the bar like jazz percussion,
storms of contrapuntal quavers

competing with the music and the girl in the sequined dress
for the room's attention. Unsurprisingly,
they asked us to leave.

In the taxi, your words were spent — or had they been mine?
The driver's eyes in the mirror were complacent,
as the silence stripped us of solidity, of outline.

And when we lay together that night
I curled you safely back into myself
so we could breed more words, lay waste to them together.

The Water-Table

On my night-walk to the city
I taste salt in the air;
the Liffey has escaped again.

Below me the vengeful sea
forms water-table committees
that mutter in the shores,

and the approaching shadow,
hood up, shoulders rolling,
could be the death of me —

like the man who'd stood
in Henry Street that afternoon,
crack-addled, screaming his love

for the children of Dublin.
Shores shudder beneath my feet
as the city forms new cracks

along fault lines I can't see,
as water rises through
hundred-year-old drains,

shell-shocked, frostbitten,
as it pours through catacombed rivers
flooding our venom back at us.

The shadow lunges, laughs, is gone.
Beneath us all, the sea sleeps
before the next great push.

III. TOLKA

Scenes from a Poor Town

Street lights turn the black world orange,
the moon is a lie the canal repeats
and repeats.

A man on the bridge agrees;
see his shape blacken the moon on water
until it vanishes.

₰

Outside the derelict convent a shape moves,
white-bibbed, sharp-beaked, the street lamp
caught in its eye.

₰

On the North Strand bombs sleep
under floorboards, below the tide-line,
nestled truffles.

Their intricacies perennial,
they glide through the night on greased rails;
the dark hours, the slow hours.

IKEA Sleep

i.m. Peggy Mangan

Miles of scrubland sub-dividing
sub-divided estates,
it's all distances here —

a long walk from Tuesday's crowds
to the blue, broken view
from the restaurant windows.

≈

To wait with patience is a quality
shared by man, woman, dog,
as is to fall out of memory,

to break through that
smoke-stack landscape,
get lost in its low-flying clouds.

≈

Her shape was clear,
among the bushes,
once we got up close.

Fire God

Touching the night with bright fingers
I travel backwards up the down-flow,
I break the rules.

On the edge of an estate, in a city
of the imagination, a horse
runs burning through the avenues.

In the Phoenix Park, watch for
my ashes on the dawn. Peel polyester
from the bone. Money burns.

An Education in Silence

for the women of the Stanhope Street Magdalene Laundry

This morning, light spilled into the courtyard
as if God had opened a window.
The light is quiet and can't be herded
from dormitory beds to morning mass —
it shines where it wants,
blushing the stained glass windows,
washing the priest's words.

My mother doesn't write.
It's been three years. My hands
crack from the heat of the sheets
as we feed them through the mangle.
The high windows admit one square
of light, on the word *repent,*
and I am silent like the sunlight.

Crosses on the Road to Sligo

At first we greet them with laughter,
with the attitude of the day-tripper —
hard and sleek as the car we steer
through these treacherous bends.

There is a hypnotism to these crosses —
an urging to recognise fatal trajectories,
the tiny slips that bring spinning wheels
to a stop. And they multiply —

proliferating now at every bend,
blind reminders of mortality,
each one its own cross-roads,
marker of a choice unmade.

≈

On our return we are quiet
and as the cloud lifts
a pale eyelid above Maeve' grave,
and roadside bouquets wither

in their plastic sheaths,
we make our own crosses,
to carry with us in the mind's eye
or on the shoulder.

The New Reality

We find ourselves in the imperial geometry
of a Spanish square; high buildings,
taller palms, the acid flash
of a parakeet thrown across

the strangely northern sky —
this icy plain that's crept over
the Iberian spring;
this home sky, this Dublin Bay sky.

We ask each other, is it so bad,
this new reality, all of us
scattered across maps without meaning,
our constant poor-mouth babble

of phones and sites
and links that don't quite
catch each other
in the acrobatic darkness?

From the shaded archways
unseen *penitentes* watch,
dead *infantas* flutter ivory fans.
The shadows they've cast

are fading into those chill skies
as the movement
of their atomic waltz
slows out of existence.

Synaesthesia

Today, every note of music
announced its presence in flags of red or blue
and every letter of your name sang its colour —
an acid-symphony unfurling in the sky.

But you're a secret and so I called your song
love-in-a-mist, Jacob's Ladder;
your name writ large in the clouds —
the rainbow.

Inner Space

Today is taken up with the puzzle of you.
Are you a star whose light only reaches me
aeons after its death,

or a film reel spinning — each frame a lost self?
Your philosophy has each cell
singing in four dimensions —

each aspect of you another Big Bang,
scattering light across a new universe:
the car you drove, the apple you ate,

your handwriting, your bus ticket,
the thought you had and its hopeful spark
racing across your inner cosmos …

However infinite you are
I have equal space
to offer in return.

Settlement

Something guides the hand
in gentle actions:

stirring tea
without chipping the cup,

polishing wood
along its grain,

smoothing flour
on the worktop.

In measuring the future
we are measured,

allowing the flour
of days to drift

and frost our
open palms,

afraid the smallest
breath might blow away

this settlement,
this home.

Lines on Your Thirtieth Birthday

We have spent some years now
filling our home

with catalogues of do-not-knows,
all our walls white

with their wash of uncertainty,
but something is emerging,

gestating its strange birth cycle —
nymph to dragonfly —

and intangible flutterings begin
in the corners of our eyes.

Inexorably, the knowns creep in,
lending their flashes of colour,

their intricate stories;
this new dapple of shade and light.

Summerhill Moon

October evening —
I ride the bus
over Summer's high hill

eye-to-eye
with the moon
in the pinching black sky.

When I get home
it's balanced on the roof
of the Ballybough House —

I call you out;
press my hand in yours,
watch the moon as it languishes

like a lemon slice
fallen from some deity's cocktail.
It's far from cocktails we are

and the moon is a bitter gift,
but a gift nonetheless;
held in the heat between our palms.

Leaving My Hands Behind

I have decided that they are partisan
or at least, not to be trusted.
For all the things they've touched, helped, held,
there are a thousand they've broken.

They're happy to be let go. Perhaps I'll see them
out and about, wearing sovereign rings,
nails painted with miniature Chinese dragons.
Maybe I'll get a wave. Or the finger.

I'll begin a new life
where a blink can shut me off,
where I will never touch, only be touched,
and I'll pull my horns in like a snail.

The Lyrebird

All day I have been practicing
small sounds of annihilation.

In the forest, not only the axe-men
hear the sound of falling trees —

me and the lyrebird stand in a clearing
mimicking the *dok-dok* of hatchets,

the banshee-wail of chainsaws,
speaking their words back to them

in our mangled patois,
because when the end comes,

isn't some kind of conversation
the best we can hope for?

Headline

All the letters escaped from the paper
have been pixilated for our reading pleasure —
no more the smudge of newsprint,

that temporary stain like a kiss
between thumb and page; words blurred
by fingerprint's maze

and that labyrinth momentarily defined
by ink that defies all permanence —
what's truth this morning by night is

privy paper (my *Ulysses* reference) or kindling
(my 1980s childhood) or a blanket for a homeless man
(that song we learnt in religion class)

and as I walk Temple Bar's rain-wet cobblestones
words glide along the channels,
dissolve in oil-glazed puddles

and shout at me from acid-coloured posters
until the technicolour blurs to monochrome
and the great unwritten headline of our century

roars from the hoarding on a derelict site:
Babies Stolen Babies Stolen
Suffering Suffering Suffering.

Egrets in the Tolka

Today one takes flight
from the shingle spit
beneath the Luke Kelly Bridge,

sweeps its blizzard wings
around the Esso station,
over the Jewish cemetary,

to the back of the Poplar Row flats —
swingsets empty
on a Sunday morning —

above me, the happenstance
of hollow bone, dusty thermal,
becomes an aerial show

by a bird that looks through me,
seeking only the shadows
of slow-moving fish.

Sackville Place

From the cobbler's shop
I watch rain
paint the pavements brown.

A smell of sealant
and burnt metal
hangs below the strip-lights.

Outside, a man
with a thousand-yard stare
shouts '*Johnno! Johnno! Johnno!*'

An old woman
folds her umbrella,
says to the cobbler:

'When you think
of the grandchildren,
you wonder:

did I ever love
my own kids enough?'
Outside, buses snort,

puddles pucker, the click
of crutches keeps time
with the key-wheel as it spins.

The cobbler smiles
and shakes his head,
'Ah no,' he says, 'ah no.'

Blackbird in Ballybough

for Tom Murphy and Jane Brennan

On the radio, the playwright
channels Spinoza —

ceasing to live, beginning to be —
when, ricocheting round

the concrete echo-chamber
outside my window,

comes the blackbird's raised inflection,
repeated question:

> *Is this being?*
> *Is this being?*
> *Is this being?*

For a moment, silence,
but for sighing cars —

then an answer comes
from beyond the railway bridge.

NOTES

'Seahenge', p. 32
A timber circle with an upturned tree root in the centre, it is thought that Seahenge was built in the 21st century BC, during the early Bronze Age, most likely for ritual purposes.

'Purgatory', p. 35
During his reign, King Henry VIII ordered the closure of a cave on Station Island in Lough Derg that was thought to be the gateway to Purgatory.

'Headline', p. 72
The italics in the last stanza quote from an extallation by Mannix Flynn, which was displayed in Temple Bar in 2013. See http://farcryproductions.weebly.com/other-events.html for more details.

Lightning Source UK Ltd.
Milton Keynes UK
UKHW012028210319
339629UK00001B/143/P